# WITHOUT YOUR FATHER

Jessica Lynne Henkle

Unsolicited Press
Portland, Oregon
www.unsolicitedpress.com
info@unsolicitedpress.com
619–354–8005

WITHOUT YOUR FATHER
Copyright © 2026 Jessica Lynne Henkle
All Rights Reserved.
Printed in the United States of America.
First Edition.

ISBN: 978-1-963115-70-3

No part of this book may be used or reproduced in any manner whatsoever without written permission except in the case of brief quotations embodied in critical articles or reviews.

This work is a piece of creative nonfiction, broadly interpreted. Elements of fiction are interwoven with the memories, experiences, narratives, and details presented within these pages. These might be characterized as autofictions or perhaps as inevitable outcomes of the inherent imperfections of memory and human perception. It is sufficient to say that, at some point, these accounts were inspired by a version of the truth.

Distributed by Asterism Books
https://asterismbooks.com/

For wholesale orders:
Asterism Books
568 1st Avenue South, Ste 120
Seattle, WA 98104
(206) 485-4829
info@asterismbooks.com

Cover Design: Kathryn Gerhardt
Editor: Summer Stewart

For my family.

And for Jack Driscoll, a spirit among spirits and my friend forever.

Are not two sparrows sold for a farthing? and one of them shall not fall on the ground without your Father. But the very hairs of your head are all numbered. Fear ye not therefore, ye are of more value than many sparrows.

St. Matthew 10:29-31

# WITHOUT YOUR FATHER

Father's Day fell two days before my father woke up suffocating. The doctors blamed a medication he'd been taking for years—hypothesized about the slow buildup of an allergic reaction—but they didn't know for sure. Whatever the cause, his throat and tongue swelled so severely that he stopped breathing and passed out shortly after waking my mother at 3:00 a.m. The paramedics arrived, but his neck was too swollen for them to intubate. Shot after shot of epinephrine did nothing. When they got him to the hospital, they put him on a ventilator and into a medically induced coma. I flew down from Portland, and my brother drove up from San Diego. We sat with our mother by our father's bedside and waited. After two days, they tried to bring him out of the coma. He never woke up. His heart gave out forty-eight hours later.

I.

1. When your father dies, your chest splits open. The devil takes your ribs and leaves your lungs exposed. You wonder if security will still let you on the plane. *My skin is in my other suitcase*, you'll tell them. *My ribs are long gone. My father is in a black plastic canister in a white bag inside his closet. My right hand is clenched tight every morning I wake.*

2. When your father dies, you move through water. Tasks that once took minutes now take hours. A scrim goes up between you and the world, and everything is filtered through it. What were you so upset about two weeks ago? What relationship seemed so fractured, what work task so unmanageable? You can't for the life of you remember. When you said goodbye to your father, you kissed his face and arms. You sang him songs. You said, "I love you." You knew before God took him that nothing would ever be the same. You haven't put on makeup in ten days, and every time you look in the mirror at your mascara-less eyes, you see him. Every time you take a step, you're weighted with the loss of a two-hundred-pound man who could fill up a whole room.

3. When your father dies, you are no longer yourself. No longer a child of two living parents, no longer, "Is this your daughter? She looks just like you." You are no longer your mission, but yours and his combined. You are life insurance calling, health insurance calling, mortgage company calling, everyone calling and telling, "My father died, my father died, my father died." Like the stories he told over and over, to make sure he understood.

4. When your father dies, you spend an hour washing your car. Twice, you hose it down and coat it again with soap. You open the passenger door and hoist yourself, wet and barefoot, onto the edge, ruin your nails scraping at stubborn spots of dirt. When you step down and close the door, you stop breathing. It's things like this that get you. Not your brother coming into your room to tell you, "He's gone." Not the first morning you woke in a world without him or the seventeen you've woken in a world without him since. Not even the number of people who came up to you at his funeral, their eyes so choked with tears, you were the one who held their hands, who said, "I know," who said, "It's okay." No, what gets you is a blotch of pine sap on your passenger side window, and now you don't know who to call to tell you how to get it off.

5. When your father dies, you hear the 911 dispatcher commanding your mother to calm down. You feel the road rip out beneath your brother's car. You hear the sound of the respirator filling your father's lungs, the glugging of the machine that cools his core temperature to freezing, the alarms that sear the air every time his blood pressure plummets or rises. You feel his palm, cold, then not, hear yourself imploring, "Squeeze my hand, Dad. Come on." Feel your arms arch over the railing on his bed. Hear yourself singing and singing when no other words will come.

6. When your father dies, "how are you?" becomes an impossible question. You pull out the bottles of alcohol he kept hidden in his workbench, behind drill sets and cans of screws, and dump them down the sink. People ask you what you need, and you tell them you don't know. You don't regret your final phone call or the last time you saw him—whole and well as he ever was—or what you said, or didn't say, while he lay dying. You knew every answer, suspected every secret smashed down inside his chest. During the slideshow at his funeral, Don McLean's "Vincent (Starry, Starry Night)" poured over shot after shot of your father's face. The song bled into another, but you stayed stuck on this refrain: "What you tried to say to me / And how you suffered for your sanity."

7. When your father dies, people are surprised to hear you start sentences with the phrase "when my father died," like maybe it would be more polite to not talk about it or even to pretend it didn't happen. As though death won't come knocking for each and every one we love, and all of us as well. As though you have the power to prevent death's arrival, or have any power at all, other than to speak the truth: "My father died, and one day, I will, too." You look those words square in the eye, squeeze tight their clammy hands. Now every day begins with these irreparable facts.

8. When your father dies, you ask your brother, "How can I go back to Portland and live like I was living before this happened?" Your brother answers, "You can't."

9. When your father dies, people try to help you. They send books, advise therapy and other methods of self-care, hold up outings and classes and activities and hobbies like they're offering a surefire path out of the dark. You let their gestures hang limp in the air. You resist making plans, resist acting like the future is still something you know how to put your faith in, resist everything but the day-to-day routine that keeps you moving, keeps you sane, or at least, keeps you suspended in what you're beginning to suspect is less sanity and more functional madness. You remember, in the hospital, the way you bristled at family friends who tried to tell you what to prepare for. *Just shut up*, you wanted to say. Not because their words weren't true or their compassion insincere, but for the stark and primal reason that he was not their father. *You haven't been here*, you kept thinking. *You don't know him like we do. You do not get a say in how we handle this.*

10. When your father dies, there comes a day when you can no longer bear waking up in a body that shows no trace of what has changed, and so you ink your skin with a songbird—a symbol of the only interest you shared.

11. When your father dies, your mother asks, "How do you go on living after something like this?" You say, "You put one foot in front of the other and keep on doing that every day." She's quiet a moment, then says, "What if I can't?" You say, "Then I will pick you up and carry you."

12. When your father dies, you lead a book club on C.S. Lewis's *The Problem of Pain*. People tell you that you're brave to do this. You tell them, "The world is already on fire." You tell them what your motorcycle-riding ex-boyfriend taught you about surviving a crash: the trick is to give in. It's only by fighting and clenching that you end up breaking bones. Let go, resist the impulse to put out your hands, accept the pull of the earth up to meet you, and you'll peel yourself off the asphalt, bruised but intact. You tell them what Deborah A. Miranda writes in "Advice from La Llorona": "Lean into the pain. / You can't outrun it."

13. When your father dies, you go to his dresser to get the gold chain he used to wear around his neck. You pull out his jewelry box, flip it open, and find your baby photos, peeking up from under all that precious metal.

14. When your father dies, your mother's friends bring books with titles like *I Wasn't Ready to Say to Goodbye* and *Grieving the Loss of Someone You Love*. You leave them in her kitchen and go home to your apartment. You pull Wallace Stevens's *Collected Poems* off the shelf. You take the book out to your deck, listen to the wind wash through the pines, and read: "The poem of the mind in the act of finding / What will suffice. It has not always had / To find: the scene was set; it repeated what / Was in the script. // Then the theatre was changed / To something else."

15. When your father dies, the world fills with water. You are a jellyfish floating on the tide. No brain for thinking, nor heart for desire. You are tentacles and gut, reaching blind into the deep. "How can I help you?" people ask, but you are pulled by a wave, opalescence and skin, swallowing all that sea-green sky.

16. When your father dies, you leave the pine sap on your passenger window in an act of protest. It would take more than ten hands to count the things his existence entitled you not to know. Like how to care for a car or make a sound investment. Shoot a gun, repair a watch, fix a broken pair of headphones. Fix a broken anything. Get pine sap off a window. What was it he told you? Something about butter. You could Google it, but you don't want to Google it. You want to call him. You want a lecture on politics and good credit thrown in. You want things the way they were—imperfect, but in place—and since you can't have that, you turn off the lights and turn on some music, swaying and stomping to Bear's Den's "Agape": "I don't want to know who I am without you."

17. When your father dies, a goblin drops a bag of bricks at your feet. "What do I do with this?" you ask. "Carry it," he says, then walks away. You know, if you ask Him to, Jesus will help you carry it. So you pick up the bag of bricks with Him, and yes, it's heavy. Jesus knows it's heavy—knows well the hurt of our sin-sickened race, which He Himself carried all the way to His death. And though you know to die in Christ leads to resurrection, you cannot help but buckle under the load. You cannot help but heave it onto Jesus again and again, though the weight still soaks you through, down to muscle and bone.

18. When your father dies, you have trouble moving him into the past tense. You keep saying, "My father wants his ashes scattered in Yosemite." Can he still want? Can you still want for him? Can you become offended if his now "inconsequential" wishes aren't granted? Can the moon fall out of orbit without the universe toppling over?

19. When your father dies, there are days when this fact swallows the earth. Worse, though, are the days when it doesn't. When you hate yourself for being more upset that you're still *single* than you are about not having a father. When you laugh with your co-workers, and for minutes, you forget you're half-orphaned. When you're angrier at the people who didn't call when he died than you are about his actual death. When you try to control every aspect of the aftermath of his passing—because no one else can tackle it quite like you can—and wouldn't he have done the same? Wouldn't that have been just like him.

20. When your father dies, people don't know what to say, but they seem to think they're supposed to. Like we were all handed scripts at birth that tell us, "This is what you say when someone dies," and they lost their copies. You tell them, "It's okay. I don't know what to say either," but this doesn't help. In your better moments, you understand that watching someone grieve is hard and painful. In your worse moments, you wonder why you're the one offering reassurance. In your better moments, you tell people, "Don't worry. I'll be fine." In your worse moments, you wonder if you even know what that word means now, or if you ever did.

21. When your father dies, you can't seem to write about the past, or at least, any part that doesn't have him in it. You are cemented in the ever-present present, sandwiched between what he once was and what he now will never be. Like someone snapped her fingers, and away your father went—a fact you must pick up and pencil into every chapter, the years stretched out before you in one endless act of revision.

22. When your father dies, you do not know. You walk around your apartment singing Leonard Cohen's "Hallelujah" like it's the only song there ever was. You step out the door and stare up at the sky, changing heat and hue with every shift in season. You keep thinking of the summer day you stayed too long at the bottom of the pool, and whether or not he knew you were faking, your father dove in after you. The sudden appearance of his body slicing through the turquoise water, scooping you up and out into the air. "Why did you do that?" you asked him. "To rescue you," he said, then let go to let you paddle off, to play mermaid or whatever other game you had concocted. "I'm Joan of Arc," you used to tell your parents, sprawled out on the living room floor. Your father never asked you why, just rolled his eyes and walked off smiling. This strange child who looked just like him.

23. When your father dies, people ask, "How are you doing?" *Not good,* you want to tell them. Instead, you say some days are harder than others, which they are, but the litmus test by which you now measure "hard" is unrecognizable from what it was before. Before this. Before everything. Before you lost your father and started glancing sideways at this "new normal" everyone keeps telling you that you'll find. You want to tell them you don't want it. You want to tell them you keep thinking of a scene in *The Lord of the Rings,* when Frodo and Sam are being held hostage in Osgiliath, caught in a battle between men and orcs. Worn and ragged, Frodo rasps, "I can't do this, Sam." "I know," Sam says. "It's all wrong. By rights, we shouldn't even be here. But we are."

24. When your father dies, there's so much there. You're stuck up to your ears in a silt of mixed emotions. Every time you take a breath, you swallow more—more of yes and more of no, more of mercy and of injustice, of hope birthed by pain and of sin so pervasive it took God's death to do away with it. And yet, it's still here, in the "now and not yet" of kingdom come, in the way He allows evil to enter our lives so that good might run in on its heels. You cannot get the one without the other. You cannot get the yes without the no.

25. When your father dies, you wonder what to think of the photographs that only show him smiling, and you smiling with him, and everybody looking like the quintessential American family. You wonder about these snapshots that just tell a slice of the tale, like fast-forwarding through the scary parts of the movie, so you don't have to watch the wicked witch—as though the entire plot doesn't hinge on her appearance.

26. When your father dies, you can still paint the picture: how he'd come home from work, set down his laptop bag and lunchbox, and walk to the kitchen sink to wash his hands. "Helloo," he'd say. "How's you?" You'd stiffen and say, "Fine," or offer up a little more, depending on your mood, knowing it would all be met with a kind but silent nod. How he'd eat whatever you put in front of him and conclude with "thanks for dinner," his praise doled out in teaspoons, if at all. You'd throw yourself down a wishing well now to make him a meal or watch him shove an entire cookie in his mouth. You'd wrap yourself around his legs and narrate every thought inside your skull.

27. When your father dies…your father dies. Your father has died. Your father is dead. You can say it over and over, in every possible iteration, but not once does it ever sound true.

28. When your father dies, you think of Rilke's words in *Duino Elegies*: "How we squander our hours of pain. / How we gaze beyond them into the bitter duration / to see if they have an end." You think how right he is, and yet, these hours refuse to be squandered—viscous with a meaning you can't comprehend, illiterate as you are in the alien tongue of grief.

II.

29. When your father dies, you go downtown to sell your old engagement ring. On the street in front of the shop, you meet a horse who tells you it was high time to do this. With your blood-diamond money, you fly to Egypt to climb the tallest pyramid, for a moment buying into the myth that this monument was built by creatures from another world. Atop the sweat-soaked bricks, you stare out into the desert, sun searing your too-pale skin. You wake in your own bed, hair and sheets wetted through, vaguely recalling a dream of your father in a coma, your father not waking, your father not moving when you spoke to him, when you touched him, your father not speaking, your father not there.

30. When your father dies, you want to tell him that you miss him. That you've kept his last two text messages and can't bring yourself to erase his number. That the day he died, you dug through the trash in your email account to retrieve the last handful of forwards he'd sent. That when he shows up in your dreams, even your subconscious understands this is impossible, and you argue with him, saying, "You can't be here. You're dead." That in these last months, you've found strength in yourself and in your family that you scarcely knew existed. That he'd be so proud of everyone. That you don't know how to be proud of yourself if you can't get there by trying to impress him.

31. When your father dies, you meet new people. They ask things like, "How's your summer going?" How you answer is not really a question. A lunch with clients is no time to say, *Bad. My summer has been bad. My father died, and everything I've done or felt since then has been filtered through that.* Instead, you say, "Okay," and make your standard joke about hating hot weather and trying not to burst into flames. One new person chuckles, but presses further. "No adventures?" he asks. You shake your head, the truth swelling at the back of your throat, knowing this is just the first of a lifetime of choices between when to speak and when to stay silent. You wonder if a lie is still a lie when you're not the one you're protecting.

32. When your father dies, a thunderstorm snaps you awake, lightning flashing through your apartment. The wind whips so hard it holds you back as you run, while a flock of geese streams overhead. It's not yet September, but the trees are already turning. All of this, and a part of you still living at that hospital, in the climate-controlled CCU. A part of you still waking that morning your mother called to tell you what had happened, and you unsuspecting, under-caffeinated, only thinking of the meeting you had at 9:00, not wondering if your father had read the email you sent him the night before because he always did, he always read them, he was always awake before you. He was always awake. It's almost September. All of this, and a part of you still suspended in June, when four days tallied the weight of your twenty-eight years, half as many as your father had to live. All of this, and a part of you in that hospital still waiting—though for what, you do not know.

33. When your father dies, a planet drops out of the sky. The galaxy that contained it compresses, collapses, caves in as it's pulled toward the void. What did you learn in science class? That when a heavenly body expires, we may not notice until years later. You find this hard to believe, hanging lopsided on your axis. Your revolutions slow around the sun.

34. When your father dies, you feel the way you imagine people feel when they get married or buy a home or have a child: you are suddenly now forever irrevocably "adult." You can't pick up and move to Iceland on a whim. You can't quit your job and take off in your car, no purpose other than to drive. In the time it took your father to draw his last ventilator-induced breaths, you aged forty years. You can see it in your eyes, the way you see it in the gaze of the airport security guard who checks your ID, looking from you now to the twenty-three-year-old you on your license and back. *It's me, all right?* you want to shout at him. *It's me.* And it is, but it very much isn't.

35. When your father dies, you think of how the rest of you should've died instead. You at two and three and four years old, when asthma kept landing you in the ER. Your brother, right before his sophomore year of high school, when his lung collapsed. Your mother, when cancer came for her at thirty-two. Not your father, who only went to the doctor when forced. Not your father, who'd wound up in the hospital for high blood pressure and kidney stones and other things that were not fatal—other factors that, when added together, did not equal death. These incidents like the earthquakes that shook Pompeii before Vesuvius erupted: inconsequential, even inconvenient, until the ground split open and swallowed all that was.

36. When your father dies, you still don't know. You sit in your apartment and watch *The Lord of the Rings* because he loved it. You turn off the TV and listen to the clock, spend an hour on the phone with a cousin who is so different from him, yet in other ways, is just like him. You go back to listening to the clock, the fridge, the nothing. You sit in your apartment. Your father is dead, and you still don't know, and you start to think maybe that's it. Maybe there is no answer to the riddle, no final round of *Jeopardy!*, no winner, no prize. Maybe the praise is in the not knowing, like Leonard Cohen croons in the song you couldn't choke out while your father lay dying but tried over and over to sing: "The baffled king composing hallelujah."

37. When your father dies, there are also the people who say nothing. When they ask how your trip to California was, and you hesitate, then say, "Not great. My father died," their faces fall. "Oh God," they say. "I'm so sorry." Then silence clamps their mouths shut. This is what you've been afraid of—the sudden drop in an airy conversation. *There goes the girl whose father died, killing everybody's good time.* You let the discomfort thicken. You don't ask them about work or their weekend plans. You don't try to make it better. But when an old car or a cute dog or a guy with a bright orange mohawk goes by, you let them point it out, let them smile, let them turn the talk back to superficial. And you realize, on the list of situations you must now learn how to handle, making people uncomfortable doesn't even crack the top ten.

38. When your father dies, you keep returning to the hospital's family conference room. The family conference room has beige couches, tables, and chairs, half a dozen strategically placed boxes of Kleenex, and no windows. Its off-white walls announce in monotone, "This is a place where bad things happen." It is here that you learn what wrecks in a brain every minute it's deprived of oxygen. Inside the low-ceilinged, stagnant box of the family conference room, your mother asks the doctor how long your father went without air. His answer ripples through your family like a shock wave. The family conference room is where you learn that your father will not wake from his coma. When the doctor steps out, your family snatches at the Kleenex. You bury your head in your hands. Even now, the family conference room still closes in around you—smothers you in synthetic shelter, pulses between your ears—your grief still breathing in those off-white walls.

39. When your father dies, sometimes, you take off your makeup just to see him. Sometimes, you catch yourself tailing a slow-moving minivan and shouting, "The speed limit is just a suggestion!" Sometimes, you can't stop thinking how your next birthday will be your first without him—all those years of a joint celebration, of lemon cake with glaze instead of frosting, and you complaining, "This is basically breakfast." Sometimes, you can't stop remembering the last time you saw him before the coma. In the drop-off zone of the Long Beach Airport, you hugged him, every unspoken word piled up in your mouth and distilling down to this: "Take care of yourself, okay?"

40. When your father dies, four months go by, and suddenly, it's fall. The leaves are fleeing, and the geese are returning, and the cold floods the air in mornings of pale gray and quiet blue. You pull on scarves and leggings and make potato soup. You don't know how, but seasons change, just as surely as God is moving you through this unimaginable grief. All this time, you've seen in people's eyes the question: will your father's death be the thing that makes you turn your back on God? As if it's somehow braver or more honest to get through this without Him. And all you want to say to these people is what Simon Peter said to Jesus when many walked away, and Jesus asked His disciples if they, too, wanted to leave: "Lord, to whom shall we go? You have the words of eternal life."

41. When your father dies, you lap your office, hands in pockets. In the evening, you lap your neighborhood, rush against the coming dark. Every day, you walk, and every day, you wonder if your father is watching. How thin is the veil between eternity and now? How is it you're still alive but feel as if you're vapor, tethered not as tightly as you once were? You lap your office, lap your neighborhood, even lap your apartment, spinning until you realize you're on the hunt for something lost. Something that was taken when your mother pressed a finger to your father's eyelid, lifted it, and asked him, "Can you open your eyes and look at me?" Taken when you realized he'd never look at you again.

42. When your father dies, you remember the funeral: how the strength leaked from your grandfather's lungs when he greeted you, how he hugged you tighter than he ever had before. He let you go but couldn't peel away his gaze, and you knew he saw your father—just as you knew that's what everyone who'd gathered there now saw. You took your seat in the front row, your mother tucked between you and your brother, until the pastor called you up on stage. The whole church held its breath. You made it through your eulogy, faltering only once. After the service, strangers commented on how adeptly your family was navigating the disaster. "Your children are incredible," they told your mother, and you lingered on that word: *children*. You had never felt like more and less of a child than you did in those days, nor in all the days since.

43. When your father dies, you go outside and lie down in the backseat of your car. You watch a tree blow back and forth in the wind. Only now do you begin to understand: a part of you died with him. You keep picturing your future wedding, walking with him down the aisle. You play the scene over and over, let it run like silt through your heart. Of a self-help book called *The Deepest Blue*, Maggie Nelson writes, "Somehow, the women in the book all learn to say: *That's my depression talking. It's not 'me.'*" But where do you draw the line? And what does it even matter? You close your eyes, replay the scene, invent a thousand more that will twist and pull away. "Well then, it is as you please," Nelson writes. "This is the dysfunction talking. [. . .] This is how much I miss you talking. This is the deepest blue, talking, talking, always talking to you."

44. When your father dies, you bleed purple and gold, spill off the edges of your bed and your desk, onto the carpet, the polished concrete, the old torn-up driveway covered in feathers and rust. You breathe meringue and ash-fall, drink the river water sparkling green algae and bronze. You sprout wings and fly downstream, collecting guitar picks in your talons. You're troubling people, half-orphan. You won't stop talking about it. Your metaphors are becoming more disturbing. What they don't know is you could tell them so much worse. You could tell them about the times you forget that he's gone. You could tell them how loosely his death makes you want to hold on—to reality, to relationships, to work, to breath, to dreams. You could tell them the thought that strangles you every unexpected moment, shoves an auburn ocean down your fire-breathing throat: when your father dies, there is no getting past it. You live in a different world now.

45. When your father dies, the world is dripping with fathers. Your bosses are fathers, their children secure, happy, safe. Your co-workers have fathers to call upon for every little thing. "You're so independent," a friend says. "I think you've been an adult since you were eight." So what do you need a father for, right? You need a father because you are not enough on your own. Because you failed each other in a thousand ways and never made it right. Because only now do you realize how much your bravery depended on his doubt—the safety net ready and waiting to catch you when you fell—and how it enraged you, his insistence on always being right. You need your father because you weren't done being his daughter.

46. When your father dies, you want to build a bomb shelter, sever all ties, prepare everyone you know for your inevitable death. You want to understand how people can act as though their lives might not disintegrate tomorrow. Surely, you, too, must've lived like this once, but you can't for the life of you remember how. You can't for the life of you remember how to behave as if it all might yet hold out. You hear yourself in meetings: "What if I get hit by a bus? No one but me knows how to do this work." For everyone else, it's a joking refrain. For you, it's something else. For you, it's the weight that seeped into your brain when your father's swelled with blood. It's the rift in your soul, the veil torn through, the half-beating heart that cannot unlearn how close we are to disappearing.

47. When your father dies, your mind devours all the things you never said, only to cough them back up one by one in the weeks and months that follow. Why could he tell everyone else how proud he was of his children, but not the two of you? Why did he fixate on the things you did wrong instead of the ones you did right? How long will you keep repeating a line from Sleeping At Last's "Uneven Odds": "Forgiveness is the lesson he cursed you to learn"? But maybe it isn't a curse. Maybe it's a gift, the way the cross was a gift, or how your resentment boiled every day until you found yourself in a hospital, holding your father's lifeless hand. In that moment, none of it mattered. In that moment, he had loved you, and he had done the best he could. In that moment, you told him, "I forgive you," and you meant it, and the struggle that has followed is you living out your words.

48. When your father dies, you sleep for ten hours, lie in bed for one more. Drink coffee while you write a letter to a friend. Pray. Listen to music. Go for a run in the oddly warm rain. Stretch. Eat. Stand in the shower until the hot water runs out. Write. Write your memoir, write about your dead father, write every thought that wells up in your battered soul. Write until you don't think about anything else you could or should be doing. Cook and eat again. Pray again. Pray some more. Pray until you understand that, though this world killed your father with its burdens and its demands, you do not have to stumble down that heavy, hurried path. You do not have to let this world kill you.

49. When your father dies, there comes a time when you have to stop remembering the hospital, when you have to forget the sound of the ventilator, push out the smells of sterility and decay that hung in the air, thick as quicksand. People rarely ask you how he died, but you want to tell them. You are a pattern finder, and you still believe, if you could just trace the threads that unwound to the conclusion, finally, you'd understand. But the end is only part of a larger tale. At some point, you have to turn around, widen the aperture, and take in the full view of his fifty-six years. You still won't find the tipping point. You still won't understand. But you'll see his smile, and you'll hear his voice, and when it all becomes too much to bear, you'll hear him say, "Don't let it get to you, baby." You want to tell people how he died. But don't forget to also tell them how he lived.

50. When your father dies, sometimes, you forget that he's gone. It wasn't unusual for you to go months without speaking, to only hear him in the background when you called your mother. "Hi Jessie," he'd chime in as he passed through the room. "Dad says hi," your mother would tell you, like his voice wasn't loud enough to travel through walls. It's going to be so quiet when you go back. You can't conceive of that house without him in it, talking to customers or watching politics or both, and if you're honest, a part of you still believes that's where he is. Sometimes, you forget that he's gone, the way you forget to turn on the porch light and come home in the dark. You go to switch on the flashlight he gave you, but it's burned out. And it's not a big deal, but it is because he can't send you a new one. He can't tell you he loves you. He can't chime in on your calls with your mother—"Hi Jessie"—and maybe take the phone from her, ask some question about your car, just to keep you on the line, just to hear your voice a little while longer.

51. When your father dies, people say stupid things. They are outraged for you, they are confused for you, their hearts break for you, and they don't know, don't know, don't know what to do, what to say, so they say anything, everything, something, I'm sorry, I don't know what to say. Everyone comes bearing baggage. There are those who believe that his death is reason enough to abandon your faith, and then, there are those who want to numb your pain so you don't abandon your faith. You have a harder time with this second group. You want to shut them up, just stop it, God can handle your agony, your questions, your doubt. If theirs cannot, you have to ask, what kind of god is that?

52. When your father dies, you think, *What am I going to do?* Even though you learned to stand on your own long before death snatched him from your capable hands. Long before most daughters knew one plus one equaled two, you studied division, learned the phonics of words, pointed his camera at everything you could find, to reframe it, reshape it into what might make sense. "Child of mine," he called you, you half-blood, you thief—stole the heart of your mother before you spoke your first sentence. She taught you the word "danger" and built a fence around you, as if that could keep it out. You climbed to the other side as soon as you were able, you ambitious one, you acrobat, you fearsome, strong-willed child. You pitched yourself far away, to places your parents had never been, and now you're here, and your father's dead, and you look back and think, *Who's the villain in this story?* Is it ever that easy?

53. When your father dies, the anniversary of your most painful relationship doesn't hit you quite as hard. This is the sole advantage of enduring his death: it eclipses everything else that ever hurt you. But what you wouldn't give to be burning beneath the sun of a familiar ache. You are a master at mourning a man who is still alive, but somewhere else, with someone else, leaving a hole in your heart that once buried the sky but has since become a pinprick in comparison to losing a man who is dead—who was there your whole life and is now simply gone. You'd be left at the altar a dozen more times if you didn't have to figure out how to feel this.

54. When your father dies, your earbuds break, and your mother sends you one of many pairs left floating in his dresser. Of course, the sound quality is terrific, and you want to tell him, *These are great, Dad.* But you can't. So you press them into your ears and listen to songs he loved. He raised you on classic rock, strummed "Dust in the Wind" on the guitar so many times, the chords still thrum in your bones. Some nights as a child, you feigned trouble sleeping, so he'd ask if you wanted him to sing. Yes. It was always yes. It was always the same song, a song whose lyrics you Googled in vain while he lay in the coma, until you realized he must've made it up. "I'll see you in my dreams" went the last line of the chorus. It was the final song you sang to him, right in his ear, in the hope that it would drown out every other sound.

55. When your father dies, you go to work and swim in a sea of spreadsheets. A comically large clock hangs above your desk, a clock it takes you four days to notice is displaying the wrong time. Since daylight savings, it's dark by 5:00 p.m. You work late, and when you get up to get water, you glance through your boss's window, catch your reflection against the backdrop of rain and empty parking lot. You glow ghostly in fluorescence, in the dim orange of street lamps, in the white wash of laptop screen—this last one, not unlike your father. Your father, who was on the phone before any of you were out of bed. Your father, who fell asleep in his armchair, TV remote in hand—the same remote he carried across the house when he woke up suffocating at 3:00 a.m. and ran to alert your mother. He collapsed, and though he lingered for four days, that was it. The future gone in less time than it takes you to drive to your office and back.

56. When your father dies, the monsters crawl out from under the bed. You can't find the light switch. There are no windows, no doors. You breathe, and there's a rasp in the room. You're not alone, but you are. You shut your eyes, pull the covers up over your head, count to ten, count to a hundred, count as if the very act of something tangible will force reality back into obedience. But that's the thing about ghosts—that time you saw a preview for *Psycho* and, for years after, begged your mother to wait outside the bathroom whenever you showered—it's what you can't or don't know how to see that gets you.

III.

57. When your father dies, you feel him judging you whenever you wash your car. "If you want it done your way," you tell him, "then you shouldn't have died." You can just see the look he would've given you. Add this to the list of things you've learned since his death: people don't seem to like your family's morbid sense of humor. Two days after he died, the battery in his most beloved car died, too. "Dad took the Acura with him," your mother said, and only she, you, and your brother found this amusing. The way no one else laughed when you joked about forgoing an urn and instead putting his ashes in the coffee can he used to store nails. It's like this, though. The words just come tripping from your mouths sometimes because you can't take one more second of being so damn sad. When you and your brother picked up your father's ashes from the mortuary, he set them behind the driver's seat. "Who gets to ride in the backseat now?" he said. "Don't put Dad on the floor," you scolded. "Give him to me." And he did, and you held your father in both hands, heavy on your lap the whole way home.

58. When your father dies, there comes a time when everyone forgets, when they go back to their routines and assume you've done the same. You're getting up in the morning, aren't you? You're going to work. You haven't been fired for hiding under your desk or responding to emails with, "What does it matter? In fifty years, we'll all be dead." When your friends make jokes, you laugh. When they talk about their living fathers, you listen. When someone says the word "suffocate," you've trained your face not to wince, but you haven't quite mastered how to stop your brain from flashing to the hospital, that breathing tube taped to his mouth. Or how to keep the slightest triggers—the words "golf" or "investments" or anything about cars or politics—from wringing your heart so hard, it pushes a sob right up your throat. How to explain that, for you, there is no going back.

59. When your father dies, you stare at yourself in the mirror—a face that is at once the same and not the same at all. You don't know why you do this, except you must be searching for some clue, some reason behind why Goethe's words keep swirling around in your head: "How clearly I have seen my condition [. . .]. How clearly I still see it, and yet show no sign of improvement."

60. When your father dies, six months go by, and reality settles in like a disease. The tension in your right hand becomes so severe, your doctor traps you in a brace. The nurse says you've shrunk an inch and a half, and you're certain you have wrinkles creasing down your mouth. "It often happens that we count our days," Maggie Nelson writes, "as if the act of measurement made us some kind of promise. But really this is like hoisting a harness onto an invisible horse." You try to act normal. You really do. You walk around looking decades older, while you feel like a girl who's had the training wheels ripped off her bike. *I'm not ready!* you want to scream. *I'm not ready.* But you're careening down the hill, hard and fast as the moment your father fell from this life and into the next. "Though I have learned to act as if I feel differently, the truth is that my feelings haven't really changed," Nelson writes. Every night before bed, you take magnesium to settle your nerves, to trick your body into believing it's not as bad as it seems.

61. When your father dies, the seasons snap from summer to fall, rock for two weeks in mild autumn, then plunge straight into winter. People pull on hats and gloves, button coats up to their chins. You think of your father, warm-blooded in shorts, and you stripping off layers as soon as you step indoors, griping for someone to please turn the thermostat down. You January babies, born in winter's nest, the buzz of cold shocking light inside your lungs. His blood, your blood, in every vein and heartbeat, in every gulp of icy air pulsing in your brain. Like the steam built from your breath—there, then not—you hear him in the morning when you sing. The thrum of his voice comes colliding like an avalanche, the treble of it something you hope spring leaves behind, when it buries what's left of winter in its warmth.

62. When your father dies, your Achilles gives out, yet again, and you're sent to physical therapy. "You're not very strong," the pot-bellied therapist pronounces, and you want to punch him in the face. But you don't, and the more he has you do, the more he says, "That was excellent," and the more puzzled he becomes. You know this look. It's the one you've seen on every expert you've been sent to over the years, none of whom can figure out why, built and balanced as you are, you keep having this problem. *My father*, you want to tell them. He lifted, stretched, and strained with little effort, but rolled his ankles, tweaked his knees, and ruptured his Achilles. You don't make sense without him, but how can you explain this, when he's no longer here? The way you don't tell anyone how you fear, when you meet and love a man who never knew him, that one day, you'll do something that will make him cock his head. *My father*, you'll want to tell him, but he won't understand.

63. When your father dies, you try in vain to tilt back into orbit. You climb ring over ring, inhale noxious gas, start a fight with Martians, just to get nearer to the sun. Stars press in around you, but their light is not the same. You're used to being blinded by a supernova glare. You'd give anything to return to that explosion, huge and silent as it bloomed to fill the sky. The weight of it, you didn't notice until it was gone.

64. When your father dies, you wonder who will sing along to the Christmas songs you play while you're baking. Who will make a star to hang over the garage and drag you outside to ask which part looks off-kilter? Who will replace the delicate pastel lights with LED monstrosities and not tell anyone until they're already wound around the tree? Who will roll his eyes when you're mock-crooning with Andy Williams, then start laughing at your antics minutes later? Lately, you've been catching yourself humming "I'll Be Home for Christmas." Sometimes, you pretend your father is sitting behind you, doing a crossword and singing along: "I'll be home for Christmas / If only in my dreams."

65. When your father dies, you switch health insurance plans. It's the first financial decision you've ever made without his input. You feel as if you're cheating on him. You sit in your office, heart beating like a drum, on the phone with a woman you can barely understand. "Is this for you or for your family?" she asks. "Just me," you say. "Are you married, ma'am?" "No, I'm not." She asks for your full name, and you hear the way you say it: first, then last, then spell the last, always, even if they don't ask. Just like he did. She still gets it wrong, still wants to put the "e" before the "l." "No," you tell her. *No. This is not how it goes. What do I know about deductibles and co-insurance and reimbursements? What do I know about being a grown-up?* "Okay," she says, "so that's H-e-n-k-e-l." "No, no, it's l-e." "Okay, H-e-n-k-e-l-e." "No, H-e-n-k-l-e." "Are you sure?" "Yes, I'm sure."

66. When your father dies, you vomit more than you have in your entire adult life. Every day, you feel yourself siphoning away, draining out your limbs like you've sprung a heart-leak. Every day, you feel people's patience with you waning, and all you want to tell them is, *I'm sorry, but the person I was when you met me is no longer here.* You don't know where she is, though if you had to guess, you'd say she's stuck in that room in the CCU, willing her father to open his eyes. You would bring that girl back if you could, the one you were before the walls fell in, and you had to start living without the only person large enough to jolt you into action. In *The Necessary Grace to Fall*, Gina Ochsner writes, "Eva is changing again. She's losing weight so steadily that people are taking it personally. Every day Norm asks her if she's angry with him and then one day she realizes that yes, yes she is and she is paying him back for being happy when she isn't, for recovering when she can't."

67. When your father dies, you know he's dead. But a part of you still believes, when you land at the airport, he'll pull up, step out to give you a hug, then put your bags in the trunk. On the drive, he'll talk about Obama or *American Idol*, whichever one has pissed him off the most that day. You'll tell him about work or writing, try to sneak in something that'll make him proud. At home, he'll take your suitcases to your room. One of them will hold the Sudoku puzzles you bought him for Christmas, plus some other random gift—mixed nuts or a travel mug or a book about Yosemite—because you didn't know what else to get him. A few hours later, he'll reappear in your doorway and ask if you need some money. No matter what you say, he'll pull out a few bills. "Thank you," you'll tell him, and he'll give you a wink and walk away. You'll put the money in your wallet and go back to what you were doing, never thinking that this scene will one day stop repeating.

68. When your father dies, you try to imagine a world in which he didn't. Where you can wait at the kitchen window and watch for his car. Where your inbox still gets a weekly dose of forwards about the merits of patriotism or an internet conspiracy or cool pictures of far-off places where neither of you has been. Where your eye doctor sees you no longer have vision insurance, says, "Oh, you're on your own now," and that statement doesn't send a spear of panic through your throat. Where the house you grew up in doesn't feel like a Halloween pumpkin—gutted, carved, and stuffed with fire—and yet, somehow, still standing.

69. When your father dies, you keep waiting to feel okay again, until one day you realize that *this*—this hollowed-out weight, this sense of forever searching for something you can neither find nor even name, this not knowing how to answer anyone who asks how you or your mother or your brother are doing—this might be your new "okay." Or more likely, it's depression masquerading as okay. Well, so be it. This is going through the motions. This is putting on a ruse. This is saying, "I'm okay," until you start to mean it. This is practicing belief until you regain faith in gravity.

70. When your father dies, it snows during the night, and the world you wake up in is not the one you went to bed in. You sweep powder off your deck, wrestle shrink wrap onto your windows, glide along to the store while most of the city stays inside. Back at home, you eat your groceries in front of your insulated windows. You wonder what you couldn't survive. You keep waiting for your self-sufficiency to run out, but it only seems to spread, the way a crack in the ice shoots clear across the road. You think of your father on the roof of the house, replacing shingles or flushing the plumbing. You think of him under the hood of a car, perched atop a ladder, hunched over some impossibly small thing he insisted he needed to mend. You think of all the times he didn't ask for help.

71. When your father dies, after a while—which is not nearly as much time as it should be—people start to treat you as though he didn't. As though you're a regular twenty-eight-year-old woman who isn't stuck in a sky that's turned to sea. They get upset that you no longer muster much enthusiasm for things. How can you explain? When your father dies, the water rises until it rests beneath your chin, and when, after months, it shows no signs of receding, you must become selective about what you're willing to shout for.

72. When your father dies, there are clear, cold nights when you look up at the stars, searching for Orion, the only constellation you can consistently find. You remember the mythology surrounding it and think, *Why shouldn't we make up stories about the stars?* You remember camping as a child, sitting with your father by the fire. You asked about dinosaurs and glaciers and the bats that flew in after dusk. Were there bears? And what about lions? And who and how and why? You don't remember what he said, just the crack and warble of the fire, the two of you craning your necks to stare into the black—past the bats skittering through your line of vision—at all the stars whose names you didn't know.

73. When your father dies, your birthday comes without apology, riding in, as it always has, the day after his. You thumb through your recipes, flip past all the cakes you can't bring yourself to make. The yellow with chocolate buttercream. The strawberry with sprinkles. The lemon with glaze instead of frosting, the one you got stuck eating year after year. Not even this appeals, your lifelong sweet tooth—one of few things you didn't get from him—supplanted by a deeper craving. "Make a wish," someone will say, candles flickering at the ready. A wish for what? There is no word for that which wasn't perfect—which, most of the time, wasn't even good—but was yours. The thing you'd still conjure back in half a heartbeat if you could.

74. When your father dies, there is the danger of attaching like a mollusk to anyone who offers comfort. You feel it like a hunger, the way you yearn to bend this situation into something you can stomach. You read a story about a woman who marries hastily after the death of her parents. You understand this, and so you tell yourself you're not a mollusk but a ship, fast and smooth as glass, sloughing off entanglements like you'd shed a second skin. But soon, you start to feel the way the tide recedes at sundown, exposing a scattered backwash of driftwood, seaweed, shells. You are that shoreline, wincing in silver moonlight, aching for the water or something, someone, anyone to come and cover what the undertow forgot to carry out.

75. When your father dies, people try to redirect your attention: aren't you grateful you had him for twenty-eight years? As though your past is the consolation prize for not getting to finish the game. But it's not the abstract you miss. It's the startling realities. The candle that cuts your breath because it smells like his cologne. "Leather and Lace" erupting from the radio, Stevie Nicks's rasp and rumble pulling you into summer car rides through Yosemite. "This writing," people ask you, "is it helping?" And in this question is another: isn't it time you moved on? As though you're getting over a man you have a shot at replacing. This is the end of the road, folks. There's no going on from here. You can't stop haunting the bends of this path, shutting your eyes to better feel its dust on your face, stooping down to press your hands to the mess of it, to see if there isn't something left to hold onto. *If you haven't lived this,* you want to say, *I don't expect you to understand. But you don't get to tell me when I'm done grieving for my father.*

76. When your father dies, a puddle of water seeps into your trunk, and you don't know if it's from the sudden snow or all the rain, or if even your car is giving up and cracking at the seams. You go outside at 9:00 at night, with a flashlight and towels, and mop up the mess. When you step back into your apartment, your heart catches—you can smell him—and you don't know if it's the car or the towels or the musk of incense burning on your table, but there it is, his scent, in a room he never set foot in, and you drop the towels, shut your eyes, and breathe, though you know you won't be able to take it all in. That night, you dream about him. He's sitting at the table, absorbed in his thoughts. You want to ask him something, but then, it's too late, the scene morphs into another, and in the morning, you strain to remember what you wanted to say. Outside, the towels are drip-drying on the deck, the incense long burned out, your car locked in the driveway, right where you left it.

77. When your father dies, you want someone to tell you, *Everything will be okay*, and mean it. You don't want to get your car fixed or call the dentist. You don't want to be an adult. You want to close your eyes and count to ten, shout, *Daddy, come find me!* Because sometimes, you have to pretend it's all a game—that this is one of his stubborn, silent phases, and tomorrow, you'll have two new text messages, like the ones you still can't erase. How these last months have toppled down like waves that crash on waves, each one distinct and yet exactly the same. Out on walks, you stare up at the sky and picture anywhere but here. Once, your father brought you back a snow globe from Florida. Every time you shook it, glitter rained on pink flamingoes, then settled at their feet. You shook it and shook it again, imagined yourself inside that shimmer, like so much improbable snow.

78. When your father dies, you go to an acupuncturist, who drops needles into your legs, your back and belly, the surprisingly tender top of your head. Sometimes, while you're lying there, seized in utter stillness, you think of what your father would say about you doing this—the money, the unproven science. It's been 227 days since you last heard his voice. You used to go for weeks without speaking to him, and now there are times when you'd cut off a hand just to hear him say your name. Times when you want to believe every needle the acupuncturist dislodges is pulling out part of the pain. During one session, he plays alarmingly upbeat music, bongos banging in your ears, and you imagine being chased through the jungle. You see yourself miming this for your father, his eyes squinting, mouth widened into your same smile. You hear him laugh, and you laugh, too—not so hard that your muscles pull against the needles, but enough to make you grin, face down in the dark.

79. When your father dies, your watch dies, too, and you hunt for a screwdriver to do the repair. Your mind trips over words he didn't teach you: swivel heads, steel blades, Phillips, slotted, plated shafts. Months before, you got a flat tire and had to stand in the parking lot, useless, as your co-workers put on the spare. For each lesson he forced you to learn, there were a dozen he didn't mention—believing, as he seemed to, that he would live forever. Would be there with a tool for every occasion, an answer for every practical dilemma. "You can't take it with you," so goes the saying, but some things, you can. Some things rip away right along with your soul. They're the things that slip out the door while your daughter watches you dying, bleed out through the breathing tube that's lodged in your throat, shut down one by one as your brain stops sending signals, the cogs and wheels slowing, the last cell cracked and pulsing, the light of your face growing dimmer, until it disappears.

80. When your father dies, you try to befriend good men. You talk to your acupuncturist about his trip to Italy. You chime in when your male co-workers bring up *Star Wars* or sports. You tell yourself not to look at them like something you lack—the way a valley, thirsty with drought, scans the skies for the smallest storm, any chance to suck the life back into the ground. You think of the beautiful idiots you tend to fall in love with, who are nothing, no, nothing like your father. Your father, strong and capable. Your father, steady and distant. Your father, who didn't pale in the shadow of your ambition, who rounded out the edges your docile lovers would never fill. Your father a wall, your father a force, your father gone the way the Romans salted the earth of Carthage, to keep anything that ever was from growing back. Those lovely, helpless men suddenly no longer enough.

81. When your father dies, you dream you lose your baby inside the television, wade naked through the sewer, hitch a ride to God-knows-where in the back of a covered wagon. In the waking world, you run a mile and bend your body clean in half. Deep go the aches inside your hips and back, so deep you have to lie on a heating pad before you can fall asleep. Tossing around in your sheets, you dream of coyotes and wake in the dark, stare up at the ceiling, and know: your father trickling out like river water, the thin line of you struggling to fill what only empties again. But still, you try, as Ann Patchett writes, "People die, terrible things happen. I know this now. You can't pick up and leave everything behind because there is too much sadness in the world and not enough places to go." You roll onto one side, prop your legs on a pillow. You call to the wolves, who edge out from the pines, silent as they follow you home.

82. When your father dies, you want the world to be fair: yes or no, right or wrong, black or white, here or gone. You want to put grief in a box, coo to it like an animal when it's safe and convenient. You want signs and guideposts, barriers and medians, so grief can't spill over when you're driving, when you're working, when you're out having fun. You want to remember the way it felt to sit in the hospital because, after all these months, it's starting to feel like a bad dream. Surely, you're still a man's daughter. Surely, he'll be there when you call. Surely, he'll turn you when you barrel down the wrong direction. But you're like a street traveled at night in the rain—lights smearing on the windows, water flashing at the crossroads, red and green and yellow blinking from one way to the next, the cyclist you almost run over because you're only seeing everything else.

83. When your father dies, it's 6:00 p.m., and you want popcorn, and so you eat some, even though it will spoil your dinner. Your grandmother gets pneumonia but recovers because you prayed for her and because your mother told her, "I'm not ready for you to die yet." Some things are just that easy, like sleeping too late on a Saturday and telling yourself it's fine, you're still a kid, you can do whatever you want. Things you're supposed to take solace in and have never wanted to believe as badly as you do now, but you can't because your trips around the sun have somehow added up to a number greater than your years. "You still have so much time," people tell you, but you know that you don't. You know it's running out faster than any of us can fathom.

84. When your father dies, you try to find him in your eyes, in the ache between your shoulders, in the heart-catch in your throat that says, "We put family first." You try to run from him in the sea spray of Croatia, through the snow-packed streets of Boston, in the downpours of Portland. You try to feel him in the muscles that tense as you lift your tote bag, in the twist of the screwdriver you bought to repair your watch, in the timbre that rises in your voice as you sing America's "Ventura Highway" at the top of your lungs. Instead, you keep him in a photo on your iPod, in the waxy soap and special sponge you use to wash your car, in the nose your mother recognized as his, even from the sonogram.

IV.

85. When your father dies, you start to pay attention to the news, now that he's not here to pour it in your ear. You read about gunmen in Paris, bombings in Beirut. You remember the hours your father spent watching, reading, arguing about the news. The provisions he piled while his blood pressure climbed, and your mother always telling him, "Enough." You said it, too, but not as often as you thought it: *enough*. Not because the darkness doesn't matter. But because allowing that darkness to sink in its talons will smother the light God longs to flood into this world. You knew it even then. How much more you understand it now.

86. When your father dies, these are the things that don't make sense: calendars, noise, getting up on time, breakfast, making plans, money, sleeping away the winter though you've done it, crows, the sudden arrival of spring, even numbers, the love of younger men, how you can simultaneously have no idea who you are but also know, with startling clarity, why you're here and what you want. These are the things that do make sense: children, bruises, the smell of fire, orchids, violins if not the men who play them, sunlight spilling through the trees, wind, weight, working to lift your spine up off your hips, dirt, glass, love that isn't love at all but something else indeed, looking into your eyes every night before bed and finding a valley of age in each iris.

87. When your father dies, you straddle a line—there's where he was, and where he's not, and nowhere in between. You are pulled in both directions, and yet, there is no movement, and everywhere, the sky is running down. Like a room that looks the same as when you last stood within it, save everything leaning sharp to the left.

88. When your father dies, you dwell in metaphor: Alice trapped in the looking glass, and it doesn't matter which side because you know it's the wrong one. It is a Thursday in March. Things are starting to bloom. These are the facts, but your brain splits them off and leaves you swirling in a vapor of sloth and abandon—one that renders reality at once too loud, too harsh, too grating, and yet, not enough to shock you back into a productive existence. Every time you try to move, you're flattened, and you slip into a shape you can't pin down for anyone, not even yourself.

89. When your father dies, grief feels like fear, sadness like thirst, longing like the bone-chill of being out in the cold. Deprivation like the hunger nothing seems to quench, aggravation like the muscle flutter of limbs too long held close. Exhaustion like burning, breathing like yearning, lust like a distant reminder of something you almost remember feeling. Rainfall like nothing, sunshine like nothing, wind like belief, if you can let yourself believe it, if you can let your skin remember air, remember sound, remember anything at all. Laughter like amnesia, silence like warm water, alone like brick and mortar, like anger, like over. And over. And over. Like reading a life on paper that isn't there at all.

90. When your father dies, Easter falls on the nine-month anniversary of his death. You spend it at a friend's house outside of Reno, Nevada, watching *The Hunger Games* and eating chocolate eggs. As soon as the cramped, propeller-driven plane that carried you there neared the ground, a deep, angry part of you let out a breath of relief: this landscape made sense, all brown and dirt and barren. Spring in Portland had become an insult, the sky sopping with blue, plants filthy with life. But out in the desert, the wind kicks up in a rage, tossing tumbleweeds over pavement, flicking dust into your eyes. You crack open a window and let it fly into the house, air electric as you soak in the tub. *For dust thou art, and unto dust shalt thou return,* you think. You watch your chest rise and fall in and out of the water, heart thumping harder the further you sink.

91. When your father dies, you give up faith in physics. There is no action equal and opposite to a definition falling out of the sky. Whatever pull human logic once had seems to snap and fall away, like a tree branch grown too brittle to withstand the wind and rain. How can you explain that, after the terror, this all became a form of assurance? "Before you know what kindness really is / you must lose things," writes Naomi Shihab Nye, "feel the future dissolve in a moment / like salt in a weakened broth." You stood on the edge of a precipice, and yes, you have fallen in. But isn't there something to be said for what you've found at the bottom?

92. When your father dies, you put on the dress you haven't worn since his funeral. It hangs loose and limp on your body, and you don't know if that's because it's spent months on a hanger, stretching toward the floor, or because your muscles have reshaped themselves into something the fabric can no longer contain. You take off the dress and put it back in the closet. The clouds collect hot and humid over Portland. They break into a small and stunted rain come evening, which stops almost as soon as it starts. In yoga, you twist into compass pose, and you want to believe in the symbolism of that. In direction. That a leg arcing out behind your head could pierce the sky. That wrapping what's left of you in an ill-fitting garment could be enough to lay things to rest.

93. When your father dies, one Sunday, you see your ex across the sanctuary. You'd rather believe he doesn't know your father is dead than that he does—that he's known this whole time, and still, he's said nothing. You picture the men who've let you go, lined up like silent mile markers as you trip back through your past. "When you are broken, you run," Helen MacDonald writes. "But you don't always run away. Sometimes, helplessly, you run towards." This has been the difference between you and them—you've always known your demons could not be outdistanced. You've always known they stay with you, until one day, out of nowhere, they're gone. From across the pews, you watch your ex and think, *I don't even know that person anymore.* You are not the same woman he ran from, and there is strange consolation in that.

94. When your father dies, you don't know what you want. You want someone to be there when you get home from work, or you just want to be left the hell alone. You want to hide in bed until you dissolve into the mattress, or you want to run for hours and maybe never stop. You want to remain lonely because it might make you more compassionate, or you want to fill your life with so much love you nearly choke on it each morning that you wake. You want a button you can press to stop the sudden, awful reminders that he's not here anymore and never will be again, or you want to shut your eyes and replay every memory to keep death from making a big man seem so small. You want to lie in a field and watch the days rush over your head. You want a way for him to see you finding all the things you might yet learn to want.

95. When your father dies, well-meaning people tell you to move on. All your sadness won't bring him back. Hush now, honey, and after all, God would rather have you bury your burdens in the basement than cast them out onto the lawn, where everyone can see. You listen to these people with an ache in your heart. You want to ask who taught them these things. Who taught them that grief was akin to shame? Who made them believe that faith couldn't crawl into bed with doubt, that joy got canceled out if it was tangled up with pain? Who told them, when their own loss ripped a cavern in their souls, that dry-eyed prayers were all the Lord could bear? You want to take their trembling hands, lean right in, and whisper, *Open your eyes, love. Jesus isn't throwing stones.*

96. When your father dies, grief gets to you by making you think it'll last forever, though the truth is, nothing does. You will carry his death for the rest of your life. This, you have long known. But what your father taught you—both by what he fought for and what he didn't—is that you always have a choice. It may not be a good one, and in the grand scheme of things, it may not seem like much. But it's there, and when you can't bring yourself to believe in an end to this unending season, you start by asking God to prove more powerful than your patterns.

97. When your father dies, the seasons turn, hot as the days when you lost him. "It'll get easier," people kept telling you, but you did not believe them—could not fathom an hour when this grief didn't gut you—and then, somehow, the sharpness, ever so slightly, subsides. How that alone feels like betrayal. You put his photographs on your laptop and mix them with your own, your lives running parallel but rarely combined. You've tried to make your peace with that. While he was dying, you sang him dozens of songs, but Josh White's "Enclosed by You" is the one you remember most clearly—your voice catching, then and now, at the opening lines: "Will you stay with me / When I forget you're there?"

98. When your father dies, you see a car just like his, and there isn't even a flutter of hope he might be behind the wheel, its windows and once-white surface caked with grime. There's no way on God's green earth he'd let a car get that dirty. It's the way you think of him every time you grip the wrench he handed you when you moved out, or how you'll probably always be a registered Republican, so he doesn't disown you from heaven. How a life whittles down to these minute, eternal reminders. He is not every Chevy Blazer. He is only the clean ones. He is the portobello on the grill beside the steak, finally letting you have your vegetarian eccentricities—shaking his head as you turn that mushroom into a sandwich, smiling with something like pride when you teach your brother to do the same.

99. When your father dies, the world once again fills with water, seeping onto the floor of your closet. Your apartment becomes a festival of laundered sheets and blankets, like the forts you and your brother used to build from couch to table. The damaged goods, you move to the deck, unable to bring yourself to throw them away: the comforter you've held onto since age seven, the pillow your aunt made out of your favorite childhood shirt. Here's the lesson: what you stow away can dissolve when you aren't looking. And here's the other: not once did you reach for the phone to call your father, that lifelong reflex washed away like winter's chill. Though if you sit still enough beside your emptied closet, you swear you can feel the damp of him, even now.

100. When your father dies, you are tired, want to shut your eyes and understand the pull grief has on the body, how it can kick into old injuries and vulnerable tendons, how it can swell between your hipbones and how your body just lets it, accommodates it like a baby, like something you were born to carry, keeps it fed on cells and blood until it starts to kick, grows too big for the space you've made for it, swells until you can no longer see where you're walking, until you feel it ready to drop out from inside you, but it clings with teeth and talons, clings like a song caught in your throat, and you're tired and so you let it, you shut your eyes and let it, feel the thick of it inside you until you think, maybe this is it, this thing is now a part of you, and maybe that's not so bad, after all, it's made you bigger than you've ever been before.

101. When your father dies, you remember the neurologist calling your mother at 7:00 a.m. and telling her to prepare for the worst. You remember waking to find her in hysterics, then storming into the CCU and commanding everyone you found there, "You take my mother's number off your charts. If anything happens, you call me, you understand? You call me." You remember snatching your mother's cell phone and the house phone and your own phone and holding them hostage in your room every night, lined up by your bedside like electronic soldiers. Nearly a year later, you rarely switch your ringer to silent, certain the slap of a sudden shock lies ready to ambush you the moment you drop your guard. These are the aftereffects, the way you become convinced the world is held together by a single string, and you alone are responsible to keep it from fraying.

102. When your father dies, you linger in a mourning hangover, inching back the blackout curtains bit by bit by bit. Where is the balance between living your life and stuffing sadness down the garbage disposal like rotting leftovers? How do you know if you're trapped beneath the boulder of depression or slogging through the normal swamp of grief? You have no idea. All you know is what Anne Lamott writes: "The great writers keep writing about the cold dark place within, the water under a frozen lake or the secluded, camouflaged hole. The light they shine on this hole, this pit, helps us [. . .] holler into it, measure it, throw rocks in it, and still not fall in. It can no longer swallow us up. And we can get on with things."

103. When your father dies, you learn of the inconstancy of love, how it can shift and change and push up over, even with an entire life to back it up. All these weeks of waking as half a daughter, blood of your blood drained clean from the earth—these are the things your heart hardens against as you place the family money in a trust, the lawyer's number in your phone. Prepared, as you can ever be, to take on that for which there is no preparing. And yet. There are still nights, washing the dishes, when the songs you sang to him come crawling off your tongue. Still moments when you're flipping through a stack of prints, and you land on one whose words slice through you like an answer—a warning that rises from your father, via Isadora Duncan: "You were once wild here. Don't let them tame you."

104. When your father dies, you pray, though you cannot say for what. You've taken to reading science fiction—stories of navigating alien planets—because it's been the only thing that's made sense. In *The Left Hand of Darkness*, Ursula K. Le Guin writes, "The only thing that makes life possible is permanent, intolerable uncertainty: not knowing what comes next." You have no idea where you are. There was a time when this would've driven you crazy, and it's not that it doesn't bother you now. It's that your faith in God has somehow grown greater than your need for control. So if you trust Him—worn and ragged though you are—you have to believe that He's working in all the intolerable uncertainty, and that He'll teach you how to live without your father.

105. When your father dies, you dream you could lose your mother instead, as a big white plane lands in the yard to take her away. She looks at you, and so does he, and you're faced with the impossible choice: which parent do you need less? Your voice falls out from under you, and just as fast, the scene turns, and you're watering an orchid so loaded with flowers, you expect to still see them when you wake. But you don't, and it takes a full minute of morning sunlight to remember all that is, and is not. To not shut your eyes and burrow under the covers, until the plane reappears, and you fill it with as many orchids as you can gather—no parents to be lost.

106. When your father dies, you keep getting stuck on the wrong side of trains. You shut off your engine and let your iPod cycle through song after song. In one month, it will be a year since you lost him. You'd like to say something significant has changed, but the truth is, your outward life doesn't look much different. You still have the same job, live in the same apartment. You still don't know how to rotate your tires or fall for anyone you're supposed to. The cars pile up behind you, the light going red, then green, then red, then green, and still, no one can move. The clouds hang over the road in such ivory-draped extravagance, it's like they have something to prove. In your rearview mirror, you watch a couple in a truck—the man on the phone, the woman not speaking—the light going green, your car still in park.

107. When your father dies, you keep waiting for the bottom to drop out, until one day, you realize there is no bottom, and maybe never was. You sit at your desk, watch the rain fill the parking lot. You wonder if you'll ever stop expecting someone to come along and rescue you. You turn back to your work, then shut your eyes, and suddenly, you're running through a different parking lot, past the ambulance, through the sliding doors, and up to the man at the front desk. "Why you runnin'?" he asks. Breathless, you tell him, "My father has brain activity today." Words you never thought you'd have to say. Things you never thought you'd have to learn: how to hold a hand that can't hold yours in return. How to redefine his place in this world as an absence. How to be living one life, and the next day, find it gone, and keep on getting up and living just the same.

108. When your father dies, the world spins madly on, and all you can do is catch it by the tail and let it pull you along in its wake. What day is this? What season is this? Who are you now? You do not know. You walk out of your apartment and think about death—how all it takes is one slip of the hand, one blink of the wheel turned at just the wrong time, the decades of stress that built up in his veins, and how they've carried into yours, and how you're learning to say no. You get on the phone, and you think about strength, and what it takes to be happy, and how we've got it all wrong. Maybe what matters are all the moments strung together, or how God's peace can thunder through the thrash of any storm. How you touched your father every day that he lay dying, and how you can no longer distinguish the minutes you clung to him from the ones where you were learning to accept that he was gone.

109. When your father dies, the black dress continues to hang in your closet, unworn since you laid him to rest. That day, you stood up at his funeral and, for the first time, spoke of him in the past tense. Still, it's the tense people notice—the "my father was," "my father had," "my father didn't" that they catch. "Is he no longer around?" they ask. As if you've made a grammatical mistake. *I'm sorry*, you want to tell them. *I should've said "is." My father is a man who, like my brother, can fix anything mechanical, tangible that is broken. My father has a way of correcting that is not easily set aside.* The day of the funeral, your mother's best friend took your face in her hands. "Oh," she said. "You look so much like your father." Your father was never fond of the color black.

110. When your father dies, you visit Lake Tahoe, stand still before the bluest water you've ever seen. It's the first time in a year you've felt something like peace. The landscape of grief has consumed you—taken the spirit you've fiercely protected and wrapped it round with stone. You promised your friends, when it was time to move forward, you'd know it. But now you don't know where to begin. And you think of the miracles of Jesus, how not once did He ask the blind, sick, and broken to heal themselves. All He asked was that they lift up their heads, reach past a world that had worn them down to nothing, and believe that He could do what they could not.

111. When your father dies, you take on the weight of him—two hundred pounds on your five-seven frame. Long and lean, your doctors call you. Agile. Acrobatic. You want to shake your head and tell them, *No*. Grief takes up a lot of space, knots up inside the body. Your acupuncturist is still chasing it from tendon to tendon. When others die, you take on their weight, too—not of the ones who've gone, but of those they've left behind. The faithful remnant, that gong of absence blooms gut-deep inside our hearts. What is this new chasm death abandons us to? Here, you are not your father; you cannot fix this. But you can describe it. You can wrap your hands around what's left to love, until it starts to settle into every word you write.

112. When your father dies, sometimes, you wonder if you'll ever feel okay again. But then, you wonder if you can point to a time when you ever really felt okay, and you can't, so trying to return to a state that never existed seems like a lot of unnecessary pressure. But something's still clearly more *wrong* than it was before. Sometimes, you have to fight the urge to crawl into the ivy that grows thick and wild around your apartment. Sometimes, you have to remind yourself to breathe, to stop holding the air in like you're afraid, if you let it go, it won't come back. Sometimes, you remember a moment from years before—in the wake of being left by a man you'd planned to marry—heading out of Big Sur in the morning fog. The clouds broke and bathed your car in such perfect light, you didn't dare try to capture it on film. For that split second, you felt noticed, and you realized when Jesus said, "I am with you always," this is what He meant: the world alive and listening—the closest it could come to grace—and you there in the midst of it, stumbling back to your version of okay.

*"Oh yeah?" Yosemite National Park, CA, 1988*

# Acknowledgements

I am grateful to the editors of the following publications, where some of these pieces were first published:

"Without Your Father, #29" (published as "Myths"), *Tweet Lit*, October 2017

"Without Your Father, #112" (published as "Grace"), *Tiferet Journal* blog, February 2018

"Without Your Father, #57," *The Sunlight Press*, August 2023

"Without Your Father, #95," *The Clayjar Review*, January 2024

# Bibliography

*The Holy Bible, Authorized King James Version.* Grand Rapids: Zondervan Bible Publishers, 1983.

*The Holy Bible, New International Version.* Grand Rapids: Zondervan Bible Publishers, 1984.

Goethe, Johann Wolfgang von. *The Sorrows of Young Werther ; and, Novella.* Translated by Elizabeth Mayer, Louise Bogan, and Wystan Hugh Auden. New York: Knopf Doubleday Publishing Group, 1990.

Lamott, Anne. *Bird by Bird.* New York: Anchor Books, 1995.

Le Guin, Ursula K. *The Left Hand of Darkness.* New York: Ace Books, 2010.

MacDonald, Helen. *H Is for Hawk.* New York: Grove Press, 2014.

Miranda, Deborah A. "Advice from La Llorona." *The Zen of La Llorona.* Cambridge: Salt Publishing, 2005.

Nelson, Maggie. *Bluets*. Seattle: Wave Books, 2009.

Nye, Naomi Shihab. "Kindness." *Words Under the Words: Selected Poems*. Portland, Oregon: Eighth Mountain Press, 1994.

Ochsner, Gina. "The Erlenmeyer Flask." *The Necessary Grace to Fall*. Athens, Georgia: The University of Georgia Press, 2002.

Patchett, Ann. *The Patron Saint of Liars*. New York: Mariner Books, 2011.

Rilke, Rainer Maria. "The Tenth Elegy." *Duino Elegies ; and, The Sonnets to Orpheus*. Edited and Translated by Stephen Mitchell. New York: Vintage International, 2009.

Stevens, Wallace. "Of Modern Poetry." *The Collected Poems of Wallace Stevens*. New York: Vintage Books, 1990.

## About the Author

Jessica Lynne Henkle has a BA in English and art history from Boston University and an MFA in writing from Pacific University. Her essays, stories, and poems have been published in many independent journals. She lives, works, and writes in Oregon, in a home filled with far too many houseplants and hundreds of books. You can visit her online at jessicalynnehenkle.com.

## About the Press

Unsolicited Press is based out of Portland, Oregon and focuses on the works of the unsung and underrepresented. As a womxn-owned, all-volunteer small publisher that doesn't worry about profits as much as championing exceptional literature, we have the privilege of partnering with authors skirting the fringes of the lit world. We've worked with emerging and award-winning authors such as Sommer Schafer, Amy Shimshon-Santo, Brook Bhagat, Mari Matthias, and Amy Baskin. Learn more at unsolicitedpress.com. Find us on Twitter and Instagram at @UnsolicitedP.

www.ingramcontent.com/pod-product-compliance
Lightning Source LLC
LaVergne TN
LVHW092050060526
838201LV00047B/1325